First Writing

Busy Days

Ruth Thomson

Chrysalis Children's Books

Open this flap to find some useful words to help you with your writing.

Contents

About this book

This book is designed to help young children with all kinds of non-fiction writing. Each double page shows a different type of writing.

On the left-hand page is an example (model) of a finished poster, report, chart, labelled picture or recount. On the right-hand side is a suggestion for children's own piece of writing. They can either choose one of the pictures as an inspiration or they may prefer to think of ideas of their own.

Reminders of things to do or to include

The writing task

The writing model

Misty is lost

Sam has lost his cat. He has made a poster to pin up near his home.

MISSING Misty

Misty is a black cat with white paws. She has a red collar.

REWARD £25

If you find Misty, please return her to Sam at 75 Richmond Street.

MAKE A POSTER
Design your own poster about one of these missing cats or dogs.

tabby cat

long-haired cat

shaggy dog

dalmation

poodle

spaniel

ginger cat

Useful words

black	ears
brown	eyes
furry	patch
grey	paws
hairy	spots
scruffy	stripes
sleek	tail
white	tummy

Writing tips
- Put the **title** – MISSING – at the top of the page.
- Write the **name** of your pet.
- Draw a **picture** of it.
- **Describe** what your pet looks like.
- Offer a **reward**.
- Write your **name** and **address**.

Words to help make writing more interesting, also useful for checking spellings

14

15

This chart shows the different types of writing included in the book.

Text type	Purpose	Features	Pages
Labels scissors	✧ To identify things or parts of things	✧ Often written as single words ✧ Usually nouns ✧ Sometimes used with lines or arrows linked to part of the picture	**6-7 This is me** **12-13 The best place ever** **16-17 What is it?** **18-19 Really wild**
Lists	✧ To remind ✧ To plan	✧ Written in note form ✧ Each item written on a separate line	**8-9 Lizzie goes shopping**
Instructions	✧ To describe how to do or make something	✧ Start with a heading that states what is to be done ✧ Use the imperative, eg Cut this. Fold that. ✧ Written step-by-step, in chronological order ✧ Each step numbered and written on a separate line	**10-11 Sally's bedtime** 5. Turn off the light.
Reports	✧ To describe things, places or people	✧ Written in present tense, eg This is an alarm clock. ✧ Non-chronological	**12-13 The best place ever** **14-15 Misty is lost** **16-17 What is it?** **26-27 Did you know?**
Questions What? Why?	✧ To obtain information	✧ Begin with Who, What, Why, Where, When, How or Have, Did, Are, Do, Can, Is, Was, Will, etc. ✧ End with a question mark	**20-21 Everyone's eyes** **22-23 What do you do?**
Charts	✧ To summarise information in a visual form	✧ Include a title describing what the chart shows ✧ Are divided into labelled columns and boxes	**20-21 Everyone's eyes**
Recounts	✧ To retell events	✧ Written in the past tense, eg We went to the park. ✧ In chronological order, ie on Monday, Tuesday or first, then, after that, last ✧ Focus on a particular person or people, eg I, he, she, we, they, Tom	**24-26 My week** **28-29 A great day out**

This is me

Abdul has drawn this picture of himself, and labelled it. He has written about what he can do.

hair

eye

ear

nose

mouth

finger

hand

elbow

arm

tummy

knee

toe

leg

foot

I can clap my hands.
I can wiggle my toes.
I can bend my elbows.
I can wink one eye.
I can walk on tiptoes.

✏️ **WRITE ABOUT YOURSELF**

Draw a picture of yourself and label it. Write a caption about some of the things you can do.

 **Writing tip**

• Start each sentence with I can ...

Useful words

bend	stretch
crawl	swim
hop	touch
jump	wash
kick	wink
point	wriggle
shake	write

7

Lizzie goes shopping

Lizzie is going shopping for food.
She has made a list to remind
her what to buy.

Shopping list

a box of eggs

a bag of potatoes

a bunch of carrots

a carton of juice

a tube of toothpaste

a loaf of bread

a jar of honey

a packet of pasta

a chunk of cheese

a tin of baked beans

a cucumber

MAKE A SHOPPING LIST

Write shopping lists for:

1. new things for school

a ruler

a pair of scissors

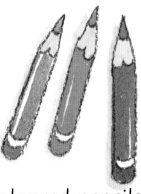
coloured pencils

a pack of
wax crayons

a glue stick

a pack of
felt-tip pens

a pencil case

sheets of
coloured paper

sticky tape

---

2. a birthday party

a packet
of crisps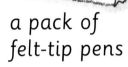

a bunch of
bananas

a pack of
balloons

mini-
pizzas

oranges

a bag of sweets

streamers

paper napkins

a jar of
peanut
butter

teacakes

muffins

Writing tip

• Put each item of your
shopping list on a new line.

9

Sally's bedtime

These are the instructions Bill gave to his sister, Sally, for going to bed.

He's so bossy!

Going to bed

1. Wash your face.

2. Brush your teeth.

3. Close the curtains.

4. Read a story.

5. Turn off the light.

6. Go to sleep.

✏️ WRITE INSTRUCTIONS

Write some step-by-step instructions for an activity.

Writing tips

- Write a title at the top.
- Write what to do step-by-step.
- Start each step on a new line.
- Number each step.
- Begin each new instruction with a *bossy verb*!

Having a bath

Making a sandcastle

Useful words

collect	rinse
decorate	rub
fill	scrub
hold	stand
push	steer
put	tip

Riding a scooter

11

The best place ever

Simon wants a treehouse like this to play in.

I love this treehouse. It has a rope ladder to help me get in. There is a table, stools and a rug inside.

✎ DESCRIBE A PLACE

Choose one of these places to play in.
Describe it.

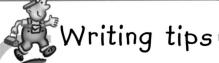

Writing tips

- Describe what it looks like.

  It has . . .
- Describe what is in it.

  There is . . .

Useful words

bell	games
binoculars	map
chart	noticeboard
chest	poster
cupboard	telescope
drinks	tools
food stores	torch
gadgets	trapdoor

Misty is lost

Sam has lost his cat.
He has made a poster to
pin up near his home.

MISSING
Misty

Misty is a black cat with white
paws. She has a red collar.

REWARD £25

If you find Misty, please
return her to Sam at
75 Richmond Street.

✏️ MAKE A POSTER

Design your own poster about one of these missing cats or dogs.

Writing tips

- Put the title – MISSING – at the top of the page.
- Write the name of your pet.
- Draw a picture of it.
- Describe what your pet looks like.
- Offer a reward.
- Write your name and address.

tabby cat

long-haired cat

dalmation

shaggy dog

Useful words

black	ears
brown	eyes
furry	patch
grey	paws
hairy	spots
scruffy	stripes
sleek	tail
white	tummy

spaniel

poodle

ginger cat

15

What is it?

This is how Rachel described an alarm clock.

This is an alarm clock.
It has two hands that move round.
It also has two shiny bells on top.
It tells the time and rings loudly.
It is useful for waking people up.

DESCRIBE AN OBJECT
Write about one of these objects.

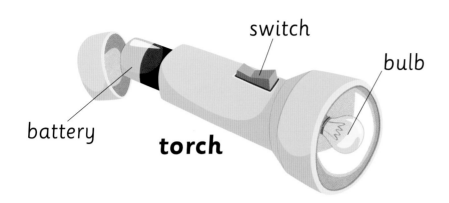

switch

bulb

battery

torch

strap

pocket

buckle

rucksack

Writing tips

- Answer these questions to describe an object:
  What is it?
  > This is a or an ...
  What does it look like?
  > It has ...
  > It also has a ...
  What does it do?
  > It ...
  Why is it useful?
  > It is useful for ...
- Start each sentence with a capital letter and end it with a full stop.

handle

spoke

umbrella

handle

blade

scissors

Useful words

hard	carrying
metal	lighting
sharp	protecting
soft	taking

winder

lens

button

viewfinder

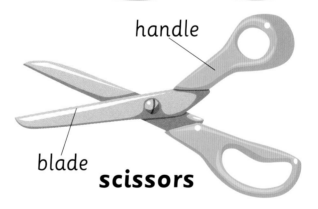

strap

camera

Really wild

How would you recognise a crocodile if you saw one? Nadia's labelled picture gives you some clues.

A crocodile

long, strong tail

powerful leg

scaly body

nostril

eye

pointed teeth

sharp claws

✏️ LABEL A PICTURE

Draw your own picture
of a wild animal.
Label all its parts.
Give your picture a title.

Writing tips

- Write the name of the animal at the top of the page.
- Draw a line from each label to a part of the animal.

lion

rhinoceros

elephant

giraffe

tiger

Useful words

furry	hoof
rough	horn
smooth	hump
soft	mane
spotty	quills
stripy	trunk
thick	tusk
wrinkly	whiskers

camel

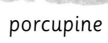

porcupine

Everyone's eyes

A class of 25 children drew a picture of their eyes. They used their pictures to make a chart to show which colour was the most common.

Eye colours in our class

Number of children with each eye colour	Blue	Brown	Green	Hazel

E y e   c o l o u r s

MAKE A CHART

Choose a question to ask everyone in your class.
Make a chart to show the answers.

Writing tips

- Write a title for your chart at the top of the page.
- Divide your chart into columns and boxes.

How do you travel to school?

by car

by bike

by bus

on foot

What colour is your hair?

red

dark brown

blonde

light brown

black

What is your favourite fruit?

orange

strawberries

peach

apple

banana

grapes

21

What do you do?

To find out what people do, you can ask them questions. Emma asked a pilot these questions.

My questions

What kind of planes do you fly?
Where do you fly to?
When did you become a pilot?
What do you like best about your job?
How did you learn to be a pilot?

ASK SOME QUESTIONS

Choose one of these people.
Think of five questions to ask
about his or her job.

drummer

footballer

dancer

writer

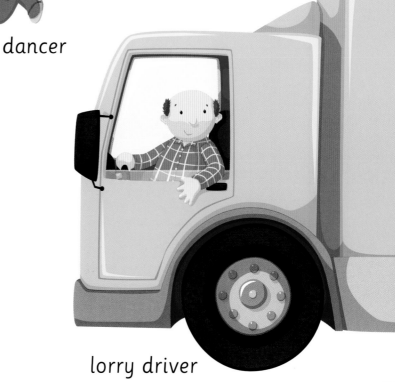

lorry driver

23

My week

This is what Alex did last week.

On Monday,	I played football in the park with my friends.
On Tuesday,	Mum and I went to the supermarket.
On Wednesday,	I had a swimming lesson at the pool.
On Thursday,	I painted a picture of a tiger at school.
On Friday,	Dad and I took our cat to the vet.
On Saturday,	I went to play at Tom's house.
On Sunday,	We all went to see a film at the cinema.

✏️ WRITE SOME NEWS

Write about what you did last week.

Use the pictures to help you.

Writing tips

- When you write your news, remember to say:

When it was	On Friday,
Who was with you	Dad and I
What you did	took the cat
Where you went	to the vet.

Useful words

had	bike ride
made	cake
played	film
shopped	friend
stayed	park
took	party
watched	shoe
went	walk

Did you Know?

Amy found out some facts about grasshoppers. Then she wrote a report about them.

Notes
- long back legs for jumping
- found worldwide, except near Poles (too cold)
- chew plant leaves with their tough mouthparts
- jump 20 times length of body

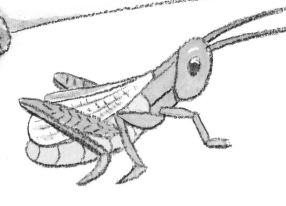

Grasshoppers

Grasshoppers have long back legs.
They can jump a long way.
Grasshoppers eat leaves.
They live all over the world, except near the icy Poles.

AN AMAZING FACT
A grasshopper can leap 20 times the length of its own body.

✎ WRITE A REPORT

Use these facts to help you write a report about ladybirds.

- ladybirds are beetles
- most common are two-spot and seven-spot
- eat garden pests
- stiff, spotty wing-cases cover a pair of wings
- lift wing-cases when they fly
- lay eggs in spring on leaves
- can lay 1500 eggs in a lifetime

Writing tips

- Write a title at the top of the page.
- Answer these questions for your report:

  What do these insects look like?

  Where do they live?

  What do they eat?

  What do they do?

  What is special about them?
- Write an AMAZING FACT about these insects in a box.
- Draw a picture of them.

A great day out

Brendan went with his class to a museum.

This is what he wrote about it.

Our trip to the space museum

Last Tuesday our class went to the Space Museum. First we saw the space rockets. Then we looked at pieces of moon rock. After that we ate our lunch. Before we left, we had a look in the shop. I bought a postcard. Finally, we went by coach back to school. We had a great time.

✏️ WRITE A RECOUNT

Write about one of these school trips.

Useful words

after	next
before	soon
finally	then
first	when

Writing tips

- Remember to describe:

When	you went	Last Tuesday
Who	went	our class went
Where	you went	to the Space Museum.
What	you did	We saw the rockets.
How	you felt	We had a great time.

- Describe what happened in order – first, next and last.

A trip to the seaside

Going on a nature trail

A visit to a science museum

More writing ideas

5. Turn off the light.

Labels

★ Children can make labels for the things in a classroom, their bedroom or a kitchen.

ball

Lists

Children can make all sorts of lists:

★ Make a list of things to remember for going swimming or on a school outing, or for a school event or for going on holiday.

★ Make lists of things sorted by different categories, such as wild animals, tame animals, hard things, soft things, fruit or vegetables.

★ Make lists of specialised words, eg for particular jobs, buildings or pieces of equipment.

★ Make imaginative lists, such as a witch's shopping list for spell ingredients or a pirate's list of his treasure hoard.

★ Children enjoy list-making word games, such as *I went to market and bought …* either alphabetically, eg an apple, a banana, a carrot, etc. or randomly, eg a bucket, a hat, a sandwich, etc.

Shopping list

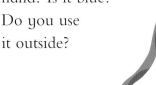

a box of eggs
a bag of potatoes
a bunch of carrots
a carton of juice
a tube of toothpaste
a loaf of bread
a jar of honey
a packet of pasta
a chunk of cheese
a tin of baked beans
a cucumber

Instructions

★ Imagine an alien has landed and wants to live with humans, but doesn't know how to behave. Ask children to write instructions for it on how to get dressed, cross the road, buy food from a supermarket or do other simple, everyday tasks.

★ Ask children to write instructions on what the alien has to do in a day, eg Wake up. Wash your face. Put on your clothes. Eat your breakfast, etc.

★ Ask one child to give instructions for others to follow, eg Wave your hands in the air. Jump up and down three times. Touch your nose. Nod twice, etc.

★ Try out a simple recipe, IT or craft activity, or game. Ask children to write their own instructions for these.

Questions and reports

Asking questions is a good way for children to focus their research, prior to reading for information about a topic on, for example, people, animals, places and things.

★ Encourage children to use the question words Who? Where? When? What? and How? For example, they could find out answers to their questions about a desert, such as: Where is it? What is the weather like? Who lives there? What is it like? Or ask the following questions about a flower: What colour is it? Where does it grow? How big is it? How long does it live? When does it bloom?

★ Play *Twenty Questions*. Take it in turns to think of an object and ask one another questions about it, eg Does it fit in your hand? Is it blue? Do you use it outside?

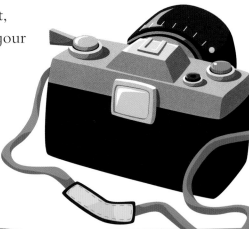

★ Play *Talk to the animals*. Choose an animal and ask children to write some questions to ask it, such as: Where do you live? What do you eat? Where do you sleep? Do you have any enemies? How do you find your food? How many babies do you have?

Charts

Charts can be used to present all sorts of information, both statistical and otherwise.

★ Make charts showing what children's favourite TV programmes are; what sports they prefer; what pets they have or want; what hobbies they have, etc.

★ Make a weather chart showing the weather every day of the week for several weeks – let children devise their own symbols for sunshine, rain, clouds, snow and fog.

★ Make a chart to distinguish two different things, eg deciduous and evergreen leaves or insects from other creepy crawlies. (Label one column *six legs* and the other *more or fewer than six legs*.)

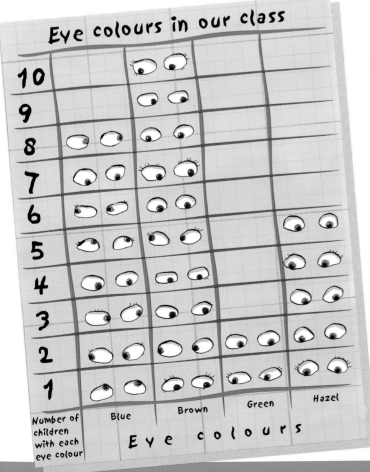

Recounts

★ Almost anywhere that children have visited or anything they have seen or experienced can provide the impetus for writing a simple recount of the event. This can be as mundane as going shopping or as exciting as going on a special outing, seeing something unexpected, or doing something for the first time, such as going on an aeroplane.

★ If you can, take photographs of an event and let children sort these in order. This will help children write about the event in the correct sequence. Using the questions When? Where? Who? What? and How? is also a good way to help structure the writing.

★ Remind children to use the past tense (with the verb ending *-ed*) and to use the connectives first, next, then, after, last of all, etc.

★ For beginner writers: ask children to tell you about an event and write down what they say. Read their accounts back to them, so they can hear what they have said.

Reminders for writing

Start titles and headings with a capital letter.

Our trip to the seaside.

Start every sentence with a capital letter and end it with a full stop.

This is my favourite place.

Start names of people and days of the week with a capital letter.

On Saturday, I went to play at Tom's house.

Start a question with a capital letter and end it with a question mark.

How did you learn to be a dancer?

Read through what you have written. Check for:

- capital letters
- full stops
- question marks.

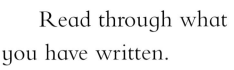